Dedicated to

Everyone who thinks they can't

TABLE OF CONTENTS

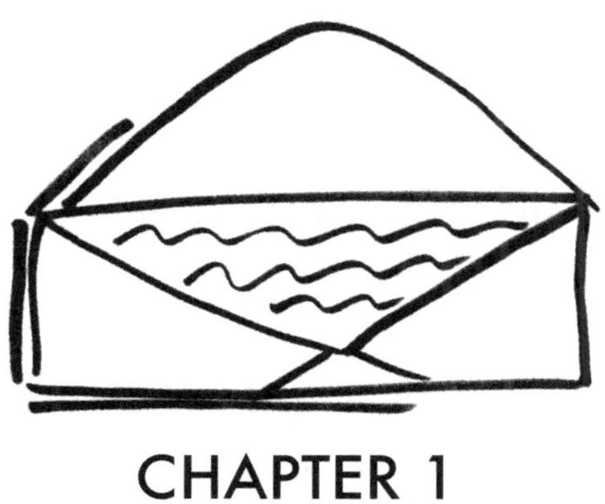

CHAPTER 1

Hi, I'm Violet! This past summer, I accomplished something amazing, and I'm going to share each and every little detail!

Rrrring! Yes! That's the last bell I'll be hearing for months! We had a party for the last day of school, but my BFF and I got into a little trouble at recess, so we had to clean up after the party. It took us FOREVER. Mrs. Wilkens said if we were fast enough, we could take the bus, but I guess we weren't that quick. After a little bit, our parents picked us up. My mom asked what was in my hand.

"It's a letter from my art teacher, Mr. Kent," I said.

My mom asked what it said.

"I haven't read it yet," I replied. So my mom suggested I read it aloud.

"Dear Violet: In class you are always talking about helping people learn and how fun it would be to teach art, so I suggest you start an art class. It will be something to keep you busy during the summer. I know you are only nine, but I know you can do it. Just believe! Sincerely, Mr. Kent."

I stared up at my mom. "An art class!?! Me?!?"

"I think that would be a great idea!" my mom said.

"You really think I can do it?"

"Yes, you are the most skilled artist I have ever seen."

"You are only saying that because you're my mom!" By the time that conversation was over, we were home. My mom and dad work from home, but they're so busy that it sometimes feels like they're not even home. After I unpacked my backpack, I took my dog out for a walk, and I just couldn't stop thinking about the art class—what was I going to name it, what was I going to teach, and what if kids cut themselves, or what if I cut myself?

After walking the little monster, I went to my dad and showed him the letter. He loved the idea! A few weeks later, I asked him to help me clean out our storage garage, thinking that would be a perfect place for the class. My mom said it was way too hot to do it out in the garage, which didn't stop me, but when I took a glimpse at the garage, a shiver went down my spine. I knew it was going to be a long day.

Half an hour into cleaning, my friend came over to help. We moved some boxes and swept the floor. Things were starting to look up already!

CHAPTER 2

The garage was done just in time for dinner. As we were eating, my brother Alex started asking about what I was going to teach during my first class. That was the last question I wanted to hear, because I hadn't really thought about it.

The next day, I asked my dad to take me to the store to get some supplies, but he was too busy. And it kept going like that for the rest of the week, until finally the weekend came!

Definition of weekends: literally the only two days we can go out or have friends over because our parents are usually free then. I know, I know: it sucks. But at least we can have friends over. I reminded my dad about going to the store, and this time he finally said yes.

Once we arrived at the store, I went to the teacher's corner and picked up

some pretty neat stuff! The next day,
I got bored, so I invited over a friend,
Rachel! She helped make flyers on my
iPad to hang around the neighborhood,
but we couldn't print them out because
our printer was out of ink.

We tried thinking of ideas, but we
just couldn't find any other way. We
wanted to make the flyers look more
professional. A few days later, Rachel
came over to see if we could print the
flyers yet, but we still hadn't bought
new ink. So we did the last thing we
wanted to do: I took out a notebook
and some crayons and tried to make an

exact replica of the flyer. Once we were done, we grabbed our bikes and started our journey to distribute the flyers!

CHAPTER 3

I was a little nervous as we arrived at the first house because the front window was covered.

I thought they were probably not home, but we still rang the doorbell just to make sure. I was pretty grateful that we checked because the door opened, and standing inside it was a little girl with golden curly hair and blue eyes. Her mom was standing beside her. We explained about the art class, and they immediately fell in love with the idea!

I was so happy that I already had not one but two new students! The second student was actually the girl's little brother!

We made our way to the next house. Ding dong! My friend from school Kasy, whom I met at the ice cream social, opened the door and said, "Hey, Violet!"

"Hey," I replied. I was so busy explaining about the art class that I didn't even realize Kasy's friend Mary was right beside her. When I finished explaining, I asked if her friend was interested, too. She shrugged and walked us over to her house, where we showed her mom the papers.

Her mom said she was interested, but that didn't mean it was a yes because Mary had soccer practice on the same day as my art class. We thanked her for her time and left.

"OK," I said, looking down at the list of people left to visit. "Next stop—oh!"

There was no one left on the list. "I guess that's the end of our journey…. for now!" So we just decided to go home after that.

CHAPTER 4

Aweek later, my dad came back from a business trip. I was so excited when he came back because I couldn't wait to tell him everything that happened while he was gone.

I was so excited while I was explaining that I didn't even realize that my dad was trying to tell me something.

Finally, my dad told me that my mom had already filled him in on everything, and that we needed to celebrate.

"So…" he said. "I invited Grandma over to stay for the weekend! She'll come in two days, so get ready!"

"Grandma is coming over?!" I shrieked. Grandma is the best! She is so fun, kind, and loving. I just love it when she comes over, so this was perfect.

I hoped that Dad hadn't told her

about my craft class yet because I really, really wanted to be the one to tell her.

Finally, the magical day arrived. "Grandma is coming!"

I looked through the window to see if her taxi had pulled up in the driveway. The minute I saw her, I rushed out the door to give her a big hug. Then I helped her put her bags inside, and we sat down on my bed in my room so I could tell her everything. She was very proud of me and asked when my first class was.

"Actually," I began. "It is tomorrow!"

She asked, "Are you nervous?"

"A little," I replied.

"Well," she went on. "Then here is some advice: don't let the world get to you, but let youself get to the world."

I stared at her, puzzled. I thought it must have been one of those grown-up riddles that are impossible to find out and never make sense. But I knew it meant something, so I just went with it.

By the time we walked out of my room, it was actually pretty late, so I said goodnight and went back to my room.

I brushed my teeth, combed my hair, change my clothes, and got in bed.

I turned off the lamp and stared at the ceiling, thinking about what it meant to not let the world get to me, but to let myself get to the world.

I thought about it so hard that I dozed off without even noticing.

I guess that was a mystery for tomorrow!

CHAPTER 5

I opened my eyes. And there it was: my calendar screaming at me to get a marker and cross that box off that chart! Because today was the day. The first class!

I was a nervous wreck, and I couldn't stop thinking about whether something would go wrong. But that didn't stop me!

After worrying, I was prepared—class would start in thirty minutes. I had been waiting for what had felt like years for this hour to come. I was so ready.

When I wanted to open the door-knob, I couldn't. I felt frozen. My grandma said, "You can do it!" The look in her eyes gave me the courage to open the door, walk to the garage, open the garage door, and wait.

I waited and waited. Nobody is going to come, I thought. I was only nine and I didn't know the first thing about watching five kids all by myself. I was so nervous that I didn't even realize I was crunching the note from my art teacher. I looked down at it, and these were the only words that popped up:

I know you are only nine, but I know you can do it. Just believe!

Those words twirled around me like the most gentle gust of wind bringing confidence, happiness, and joy. I closed my eyes and thought of the art class going splendidly.

When I opened my eyes, there were

the kids sitting down at the table. Based on what I saw in my head, I wanted to mirror it into reality!

The class started, and everything went fine just like how I pictured it. I taught the kids how to sculpt with clay. They laughed, they played, and they made beautiful artwork. The best thing about it was that they were having fun.

I was very happy, and I couldn't wait for round two!

CHAPTER 6

A few days passed, and I was really confident for the next class. Well…almost really confident. I was standing outside the garage waiting, and I thought I saw the first three kids coming, but instead, they were the neighborhood bullies. They had seen some flyers that I'd put up when I finally got some ink. And I guess they were just dying to come and tease me because that's exactly what they did.

They were biking toward me. My heart dropped as I saw them throw their bikes on to my lawn and start waking up to me.

Mark, the leader, taunted, "Can I sign up, Miss Teacher, or are you just going to bore me to death with your horrible art skills?"

The next one agreed, saying, "Yeah, I don't know why people waste their money here to watch you teach them the most boring thing in the world."

I wanted to yell at them—scream, even—that art is beautiful. It helps people express their feelings and is just plain fun. It doesn't even matter if someone is good or bad; it just matters how they feel.

But I couldn't speak up. I felt like there was a lump in my throat. I couldn't even tell them to leave. I just stood there hanging my head down in sadness. They finally left.

Maybe I should just shut down the art class, I thought to myself. Maybe I really am a bad artist.

Surprisingly, Rachel popped out of the bushes at that very moment. She had heard almost everything, and she wanted to cheer me up!

Rachel was such a good friend. She said that those boys didn't even know what they were talking about, and if they even tried, they wouldn't be able to draw a straight line.

She chuckled and added, "You are a great teacher, and the things you teach are not boring at all. They're actually fun, and those boys are just trying to bring your courage down. But that's not gonna stop you, right?"

She held her pinky out, and I guess she was trying to make that a promise. Of course, I held my pinky out, too, and we shook them.

She looked at me and said, "Now it's official, nobody will ever bring you down. You will just keep on rising up, OK?"

"OK," I replied.

As she took a seat, I let what she said sink in. I wouldn't let those boys stop me. The words that she said gave me courage, and I would keep that courage. By that time, the rest of the kids were already there, so I started the lesson. Today, I was talking about abstract art, and once they started drawing, I started thinking about what my grandma said: "Don't let the world get to you, but let yourself get to the world."

I still can't figure it out, but I know I will soon.

CHAPTER 7

I went out to the art room a little early, just to take in all that I had accomplished. By this point, I'd taught five full classes with a bunch of first and second graders, with no parental supervision. After the first two classes, I lived up to my promise not to let anyone pull me down, and I had found lots of happiness.

Today was the last class. I was pretty bummed out, but I'd had so much fun that I knew I was going to do it again. Since it was the last class, I thought I would do something really fun.

At the very end, I planned to do an award ceremony. I had bought some certificates that needed names to be filled out. I wanted to give the students something to show them that they had improved their art skills—even if they were not the best, they had definitely improved. I'm not sure if it was even me who made them improve; I think it was just a little push, a little bit of courage—just like how Rachel and everybody else had been there for me on this journey. There were ups and downs, but in the end, it was all just a lifelong memory.

Giving out certificates wasn't the only thing. I had also planned a party! We had ordered pizza, and I had decorated the classroom the day before.

The classroom was super festive. There were streamers hanging from the ceiling, and balloons in every corner. I knew the kids would just love it.

The first batch of kids came, then the second, and once everyone was there, the party began!

Everything was going fine, just how I planned it. Pizza came on time, and the kids' joyful laughs and smiles told me that they were having a great time!

Then, it was time for the ceremony. I told all the kids to come, and I gave them each a certificate. Then, it was finally time for a fun game I made up during the first class: Chalk Wars!

Each kid took three colors of chalk, I gave them a theme, and they drew something related to it. I would pick three winners.

Before we started, one of the bullies came up to me.

I said in the most polite way possible, "What are you doing here?"

He said, "I am sorry about all the mean things I said to you. I actually want to learn about art."

I replied, "That's okay. Just remember these words: 'Don't let the world get to you, but let youself get to the world.'"

I looked over my shoulder to see my grandma standing in the doorway. She nodded at me, and I nodded back.

Although I haven't found out the full meaning of my grandma's riddle, here is something I did find out: You can do anything; you just need to simply try. That is something I learned throughout this journey.

Just remember this, it might be the end for me, but it's just the beginning for you.

AUTHOR'S NOTE

Hi! I'm Venya Raju, and I am actually very similar to Violet. This book is based on a true story about an unforgettable summer when I was nine. This the first book I've written, and I couldn't have done it without my family and my amazing guide, Jeff Goins!

I wrote this book to inspire all. We all have fears big and small. To other people our fears are like a small itch, but to us it's a big storm in our head that just prevents us from taking the next leap. We all can leap over these obstacles but most fail to try. Fear is all in our head, you just need to simply try and you'll be surprised!

Don't let the world
get to you,
but let yourself
get to the world.

Scribble your own thoughts and ideas here!

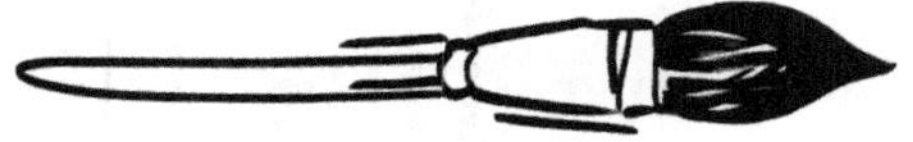

Scribble your own thoughts
and ideas here!

Scribble your own thoughts and ideas here!

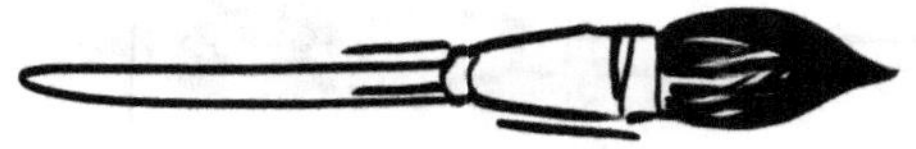

Scribble your own thoughts and ideas here!

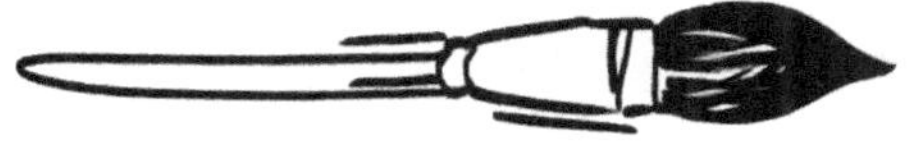

www.ingramcontent.com/pod-product-compliance
Lightning Source LLC
Chambersburg PA
CBHW051012050726
47592CB00007B/2821

JUST TRY

YOU'LL BE SURPRISED

Venya Raju

Based on a true story.

Text © 2020 Venya Raju
Illustrations © 2020 Pamela Fernuik Hodges

Editor: Chantel Hamilton
Book design by: Pamela Fernuik Hodges